Content

D0441957

Game Finder

Game	Page number	Equipment	Number of players
All It	77	1 small stability ball per player	Any number
Balancing Act	24	1 stability ball per player	Any number of pairs
Ball Hug	8	1 stability ball per pair	Any number of pairs
Ball Is in Your Court	86	1 stability ball per player and 1 tennis ball per group	Any number
Ball Safe	70	3 stability balls and 1 pool noodle per 10 players	Any number
Ball Tag	78	1 extra-small stability ball per game	10 to 15 per game
Balls Away	116	1 stability ball and 50 tennis balls per 10-15 players and tape	10 to 15 per stability ball
Bounce and Follow	40	1 stability ball and 2 cones per team	Teams of 3
Bouncing Body Ball	132	1 stability ball per player, and 1 Body Ball and 2 Body Ball vests per game	2 teams of 5 to 9
Butt-Sit-Pass	6	1 stability ball per pair	Any number of pairs
Carry the Crown	34	1 stability ball and 1 towel per pair	Any number of pairs
Cat and Mouse	118	2 stability balls of different colors	At least 2 teams of at least 8 (preferably more players per team)
Circle Relay	54	1 stability ball per team	Teams of 4 to 6
Circular Moving Sidewalk	112	1 stability ball per group	At least 10 per group
Circus Toss and Catch	92	1 stability ball per player	Any number
Clear the Deck	84	1 stability ball per player	Any number
Consecutive One-Bounce Passes	25	1 stability ball per pair	Any number of pairs

Game	Page number	Equipment	Number of players
Crab Soccer	122	1 stability ball per game and 4 cones to identify 2 goals	2 teams of 5 to 10
Crab Walk Relay	48	1 stability ball and 1 cone per team	Teams of 3 or 4
Crazy-Eights Dribble	36	1 stability ball per player and 2 cones per games	5 to 10 (or more if you make a larger course)
Dribble Relay	56	1 stability ball and 4 cones per team	Teams of 3 or 4
Dribble Tag	75	1 stability ball per player and 1 pool noodle for the It	Any number
Eight-Beat Musical Routine	108	1 stability ball per dancer, a CD (choose music with a strong beat and a clear eight count), and a CD player	Any number
Feet Pass	111	1 stability ball per group	Groups of 4 to 6
Field Meet	93	One 20-yard or 20-meter measuring tape for each throwing event and one 5-yard or 5-meter measuring tape for the high jump, at least one small stability ball per station (the game is more active if there is one ball per two players; one player completes the activity while the other measures the distance)	2 to 6 to a station
Fit Circle	136	1 stability ball per team	Teams of 5, 7, 9, 11, or 15
Foosball	130	4 cones and 2 stability balls per game	2 teams of 3 to 15
Football	38	1 stability ball per team	Teams of 4 to 6
Four Square (King's Court)	82	1 stability ball	4 to 7 per game

(continued)

Game Finder *(continued)*

Game	Page number	Equipment	Number of players
Frozen Tag	74	1 stability ball per 20 players and 1 pool noodle for each It	Any number
Gutter Ball	113	1 stability ball per group	Groups of 12 to 30
Ha Ha Dribble	16	1 stability ball per pair	Any number of pairs
Help	80	1 stability ball and 4 cones per group	4 per game
Hoops	124	1 hula hoop per team, 1 stability ball, and tape to mark two circles	2 teams of 3 to 6
Island Tag	72	1 stability ball per player	Any number
Jog Toss	102	1 stability ball per player and 4 cones	Any number
Keep Away in My House	128	1 stability ball per game	2 teams of 4 to 6
Lapping the Ball	120	1 stability ball	2 teams of 5 to 30
Last One Tagged It	66	1 stability ball per player	Any number
Le Mans 24-Lap Relay	64	1 stability ball per team and 4 cones per game	Teams of 2 or 3
Look, Mom . . .	14	1 stability ball per pair	Any number of pairs
Mercury, Venus, Earth, and Mars	42	1 stability ball per player and 16 cones	Depends on the size of the solar system, but 4 to 6 players at a time is ideal
Musical Balls	91	1 stability ball for every 2 players, a CD player, and a CD of lively music	Any number
Not in My House	126	Approximately 1 stability ball per player	Any number
Over the Top	98	1 stability ball per group	Groups of 4 to 10
Over and Under	100	1 stability ball per group	Groups of 4 to 6
Over, Under, and Around Relay	50	1 stability ball per team	Teams of 3 to 5

Game	Page number	Equipment	Number of players
Parachute Roll	95	1 stability ball and 1 parachute per group	10 to 20 (or more if you have a larger parachute)
Pass the Ball	90	1 stability ball per group, a CD player, and a CD of lively music	Any number; groups of 10 to 15 are ideal
Pass the Egg	106	1 stability ball per group	Groups of at least 4
Pass, Floor, Pass	44	1 stability ball per pair	Any number of pairs
Pass Relay	58	1 stability ball per 3 players	Any number of three-somes
Pressure Tag	76	1 stability ball per pair of players and 2 pool noodles per pair of Its	Any number
Pursuit Tag	68	1 stability ball per player and 8 cones	5 to 20
Roll the Rails	104	1 stability ball per group	At least 10 per group
Rolling Bulldogs	94	1 stability ball for every 10 players	5 to 30
Round the One-Minute Clock	4	1 stability ball per pair	Any number of pairs
Running Triangles	45	1 stability ball and 3 cones per pair	Any number of pairs
Seated Bounces	20	3 stability balls per pair	Any number of pairs
Set	10	1 stability ball per pair	Any number of pairs
Stretch	88	1 stability ball for every 2 players, a CD player, and a CD of slower music	Any number
Sweeper Relay	60	1 towel and 1 stability ball per team	Teams of 3 or 4
Target Relay	52	1 stability ball and 1 inner tube or ball stand per team	Teams of 3 to 5
Toss in the Towel	22	1 stability ball and 2 towels for each group of 4	Groups of 4
Twin Races	30	1 stability ball per pair	Any number of pairs

(continued)

Game Finder *(continued)*

Game	Page number	Equipment	Number of players
Two-Player Bowling	12	1 stability ball and 5 cones per pair	Any number of pairs
Two-Player Juggle	2	3 stability balls	Any number of pairs
Ultimate Stability Ball	134	1 small stability ball per game	2 teams of 3 to 5
Wall Bounce	32	1 stability ball per team	Teams of 2 to 4
Wall Passes	18	1 stability ball, 1 chair (or a pair of cones) per pair, and a wall	Any number of pairs
Wall Roll Relay	62	1 stability ball per team	Teams of 3 to 5
Watermelon Toss	110	1 stability ball per group	Groups of at least 4
World Cup Race	28	1 extra-large stability ball per team and 4 cones	Teams of 2 to 5

Preface

The idea of writing *Having a Ball: Stability Ball Games* came at a fitness conference in Canada where I was leading workshops on children's games for fitness leaders. During the conference, I realized the unique needs of professionals at fitness centers and the many opportunities they have to reach elementary and high school kids. Smaller exercise rooms and lots of stability balls are readily available at these centers, but gymnasium sorts of games do not always work easily in this environment. The games in this book are designed with fitness centers in mind, but classroom teachers and recreation leaders can also use them easily in small rooms or in large gymnasiums.

Stability balls are common pieces of equipment at most fitness clubs and recreation centers and in many schools. Rather than try to have kids do adult activities on these balls, you can encourage them to be kids and enjoy some fun games during which they will unwittingly do all kinds of exercise. The games in this book make you look good for engaging the children in positive and fun experiences, make parents happy because their kids have been actively engaged in healthy physical activity, and let kids participate in fun and active games that improve their health. Everyone is a winner!

FUN AND ACTIVE PARTICIPATION FOR ALL!

Promoting fun and active participation for all children is a valuable goal, and it is the goal of the games in this book. One of the best ways to accomplish this goal is to involve players in games that do not use traditional equipment. A stability ball is perfect because few people have played games with them. This unique piece of equipment creates a level playing field, which encourages everyone to participate with intensity and fun.

Fun

Fun is the first goal of this book. We can all remember moments of outrageous fun and laughter when we got lost in a crazy game. These moments of joviality lessen anxiety and inclination to depression as well as enhance the feeling of well-being. This joy is a gift we offer to participants of fun and active games, such as those found in this book.

Activity

Activity is the second goal of this book. Most of the games in *Having a Ball* are very active. Active lifestyles help all people optimize their health and enjoyment of life. On the flip side, we have all read and heard the statistics on obesity around the world as well as the growing amount of time people spend in front of television and computer screens. Fun and active games are part of the solution in combating the ill effects of inactivity, especially for children.

HOW THIS BOOK IS ORGANIZED

The book's seven chapters are organized by the nature of the activities and the number of players. Chapter 1, Partner Challenges, involves two people working together to complete challenges, such as juggling. Chapter 2, Races, involves individuals, pairs, or small groups trying to complete tasks as quickly or as often as possible, such as dribbling around four "planets." Chapter 3, Relays, involves three or four players individually taking turns moving with a stability ball or working as a team to overcome a challenge more quickly or more often than other teams. These relays include such events as a Le Mans race, in which players take turns dribbling around a "race track." Chapter 4, Tag Games, involves "Its" chasing others, who try to avoid getting tagged. The games in chapter 5, Group Games, are played with larger groups of people, and players change roles depending on the way the game progresses; Rolling Bulldogs is an example. Chapter 6, Group Challenges, involves groups of players trying to meet challenges, such as rolling a stability ball around a parachute. Chapter 7, Team Games, has two teams competing against each other, as in Crab Soccer, in which two teams try to score on each other's goals.

HOW THE GAMES ARE ORGANIZED

I present each game to help you get a quick idea of how it works. Game descriptions begin with the game name and an objective. These are followed by a list of equipment, the number of players, and the setup required for each game in easy-to-read formats. The instructions take you sequentially through explaining the game to the players. Finally, many of the games have variations, which, along with some tips about the games, are listed at the ends of the game descriptions. Be sure to look for opportunities to add your own variations to make the games work even better for your situation, and encourage your players to do the same. An alphabetized game finder is provided at the beginning of the book, which makes it easy for you to find the games the kids love so much.

I intentionally did not specify appropriate ages for any of the games because people of all ages can play almost any of the games. However, as mentioned earlier, you might need to add a variation or extra challenge to a simple game to make it work for people with greater abilities. Consider the game Duck, Duck, Goose, which is often played in kindergarten. What happens if the players are required to stand and dribble stability balls while a couple of players go around the circle? You may then add a variation in which you number players 1 through 3, and while a duck and goose run around, all the number 1s switch places. And all of this is done while dribbling stability balls! Even elite basketball teams would find this version of Duck, Duck, Goose challenging. With some creativity, you can adapt any game to grab the interest of people of any age and ability.

HAVE A BALL!

For almost all the games in this book, an extra-small stability ball is the easiest to play with, and an extra-large ball is the most difficult. You will need to judge your players' ages and abilities to determine which ball size is most suitable for them. If you have a variety of abilities in your group, you may want to equalize teams by balancing the age and ability levels across all the teams, or you may want to separate the levels and give the more skilled teams larger stability balls to compete with. The following are sizes of stability balls:

- Extra-small: 18 inches (45 cm)
- Small: 22 inches (55 cm)
- Medium: 26 inches (65 cm)
- Large: 30 inches (75 cm)
- Extra-large: 34 inches (85 cm)

Some of the games refer to BOSU Ballast Balls. These balls are stability balls with some loose filling added inside them and are sure to add even more interest to some of the throwing games.

Here are some things to consider before choosing a game for your group to play:

- Shorter games and challenges can often be repeated several times.
- The quicker you get the next stability ball game going, the more active your players will be and the less they will focus on who wins and loses.
- Having some music going during most of these games often helps to create an active and fun environment.

Having a Ball will help you make a positive difference in the lives of children by getting everybody in your group to move while participating in fun games. By using the games in this book, you will bring the benefits of activity and fun to those you lead.

Acknowledgments

The encouragement I received from Jake Randot and Mike Bates from Human Kinetics in Canada to present several workshops at the Canadian fitness professional conference CanFitPro was the impetus for this book. At the conference I presented children's games that make their experiences at fitness centers active and fun. After one of those presentations, I met Carol Murphy from Resist-A-Ball, who encouraged me to think about writing a book of games using stability balls. Thanks to the encouragement of you three, this book finds its beginning!

Gayle Kassing from Human Kinetics in the United States caught my vision and encouraged its publication. As always, Gayle, thanks for your support! Amy Stahl does excellent editorial work and is a joy to work with. Thanks again, Amy!

We took the pictures in this book with students from Prince of Wales School in inner-city Hamilton, Ontario. Heather Gardner was the teacher who made those arrangements possible. The students who allowed me to take their pictures were an absolute delight to work with. Their names are Alyssa, Chobaojmauth, Cynthia, Elias, Enky, Karen, Katelyn, Korina, Marissa, Raquel, Ruby, and Shalynn. Laura Troccoli-Ormond, director at Norman Pinky Lewis Recreation Centre, graciously allowed us to use one of the centre's rooms for our photo sessions. To all of you, thanks so much!

Christine DeBrouwer, one of my students at Redeemer University College, went through all the games, helped with some initial editing, and assisted in a major way during the photo sessions with the children. Christine, your work is greatly appreciated. Doug Needham is my dean and thankfully always encourages me to play more. Thanks, Doug!

The real thanks go to you folks who use this book to make a positive difference in the lives of children. Thank you, and blessings on your work.

Partner Challenges

Most of the games in this chapter have two players cooperating to achieve a common goal. For example, players count how many times they can set a ball to each other as in volleyball or pass a ball back and forth while sitting against a wall, or they see how long they can juggle three stability balls between them. In a couple of challenges they compete with each other or against other pairs (to determine which pair can complete a task the quickest). If you have a lot of players, just pair them all up and enjoy the fun activities in this chapter.

Two-Player Juggle

Objective

For two players to cooperatively juggle three balls together as long as possible

Equipment

Three stability balls

Number of Players

Any number of pairs

Setup

- Two players stand opposite each other.
- One player holds one ball; the other player holds two balls (or has the second ball on the floor immediately in front of her).

Instructions

1. The player with two balls throws one ball to the player with one ball.
2. Before the player with one ball catches the thrown ball, she tosses her ball to the first player.
3. Before the first player catches the thrown ball, she tosses the second ball to the first player.
4. Players continue juggling balls for as long as possible.

Tips and Variations

- Players begin by tossing one ball back and forth so that the ball is on a nearly straight-down trajectory when it is caught. Then introduce a second ball and have them learn to toss two balls. Then add the third.
- Side-by-Side Two-Player Juggle: Players stand side-by-side and juggle the balls (this is considerably more challenging than standing opposite each other).

Round the One-Minute Clock

Objective

To move a ball around two people as many times as possible in one minute

Equipment

One stability ball per pair of players

Number of Players

Any number of pairs

Setup

- Two players sit back-to-back with their legs straight in front of them.
- Give one player a stability ball.

Instructions

1. On your signal to begin, the player with the ball passes it around his side in a clockwise rotation to his partner. The partner takes the ball, moves it in front of his body, and passes the ball around his side in a clockwise rotation back to his partner.
2. Each time the first player receives the ball counts as one rotation.
3. The winning pair is the one that gets the ball to rotate around the two players the most times in a set amount of time, or is the first pair to complete 10, 20, or 30 rotations. Have players call out the number of rotations each time they complete one.

Tips and Variations

- Standing Round the One-Minute Clock: Played the same as Round the One-Minute Clock except that players are standing back-to-back.
- Using a BOSU Ballast Ball will add balance and strength components to the game.

Butt-Sit-Pass

Objective

For two players to count how many successive passes they can do in one minute

Equipment

One stability ball per pair of players

Number of Players

Any number of pairs

Setup

- Players sit parallel to each other about one to three paces apart and face opposite directions. Their knees are bent and their heels are on the ground.
- One of the players holds a ball along her side on the ground as far away from her partner as possible.

Instructions

1. On your signal to begin, both players lift their hands off the ground (the only parts of their bodies that are on the ground are their buttocks and heels).
2. The player with the ball pulls it across her body and passes it to her partner.
3. If the hand of either player touches the ground, they must begin their pass count again at zero.
4. The pair who makes the most successive passes in one minute wins.

Tips and Variations

- Allow a bounce after each pass.
- The farther players are from each other, the more challenging the activity is.
- To make this activity more challenging, players may have only their buttocks on the ground (heels are off the ground; see photo on page 6).
- Use a BOSU Ballast Ball to make this activity even more challenging.

Ball Hug

Objective

To take a ball away from an opponent or force an opponent to move his feet

Equipment

One stability ball per pair

Number of Players

Any number of pairs

Setup

- Players stand opposite each other.
- Each pair holds a ball between them.

Instructions

1. Players count "One, two, three, start."
2. On the signal to start, players try to pull the ball away from their opponents or force their opponents to move their feet. The player who loses the ball or moves his feet first loses.
3. Players play the best of five and then challenge different partners.

Tips and Variations

Kneeling Ball Hug: Players kneel opposite each other and hold on to the ball. Each player tries to take the ball away from his opponent or force his opponent to lose his balance. The player who loses the ball or loses his balance first loses the game.

Set

Objective

For two players to set a stability ball between them as many successive times as possible in one minute

Equipment

One stability ball per pair of players

Number of Players

Any number of pairs

Setup

- Players stand facing a partner with one player holding a stability ball in front of her head.
- The other player stands with her hands up about 5 inches (13 cm) from the ball.

Instructions

1. On your signal to begin, the player with the ball uses a volleyball set to pass the ball to her partner. The partner immediately sets the ball back.
2. Players keep setting the ball back and forth and count the number of successive times they set the ball.
3. If the ball drops to the ground, the players retrieve the ball and begin their setting and counting from zero.
4. At your signal to stop, players determine which pair has the highest number of successive sets. That pair is the winner.

Tips and Variations

Sitting Set: Played the same as Set except that players play from seated positions.

Two-Player Bowling

Objective

For each pair of bowlers to knock over or move five cones before any other pair does

Equipment

- One stability ball per pair of players
- Five cones per pair of players

Number of Players

Any number of pairs

Setup

- The first bowler from each pair stands behind a starting line with a ball.
- In front of each bowler, place five cones in a V shape pointing to the bowler, with each cone at least one pace back from the next one. The cones should be at least 10 paces from the bowler. The second player stands behind the cones.

Instructions

1. On your signal to begin, the first bowler rolls his ball toward the cones.
2. The player behind the cones tosses any pins knocked over or touched by the ball behind the remaining cones.
3. The player behind the cones then takes the ball to the starting line and aims at the remaining cones while the first bowler takes his place behind the cones.
4. Players continue to alternate until all the cones are removed.

Tips and Variations

- Automated Bowling: One player remains the bowler. A partner rolls the ball back and removes cones that the bowler has knocked down or touched.
- If you have real bowling pins, use them and remove only those that are knocked down.

Look, Mom . . .

Objective

For a pair of players to carry a stability ball across a room without dropping it and without using their arms or hands

Equipment

One stability ball per pair of players

Number of Players

Any number of pairs

Setup

- Paired players stand at one wall.
- Each pair has a stability ball.

Instructions

1. Players think of and count each unique way they can carry a ball between them without using their arms or hands (hands and arms can be used initially to get the ball in place).
2. Players must travel from one end of the room to the other, and then explore a different way to cross back.
3. The pair with the highest number of different ways to carry the ball wins the challenge.

Tips and Variations

- To move the activity along, specify a time limit, such as three to five minutes.
- To increase the activity level, specify that each crossing must take less than 10 seconds.
- Have players demonstrate their most original carry.

Ha Ha Dribble

Adapted from J. Byl, H. Baldauf, P. Doyle, and A. Raithby, 2007, *Chicken and Noodle Games: 141 Fun Activities With Innovative Equipment.* (Champaign, IL: Human Kinetics), 225.

Objective

To have a partner perform as much activity as possible

Equipment

One stability ball per pair of players

Number of Players

Any number of pairs

Setup

- All players line up with their partners along one side of the room.
- Each pair has a ball.

Instructions

1. Each pair of players plays a game of Rock, Paper, Scissors to determine who does the activities.
2. In Rock, Paper, Scissors, each player holds one hand under his armpit. Together they hop three times. When they land for the third time, each player pulls out his hand and either makes a fist (rock), shows a flat hand (paper), or holds two fingers out (scissors).
3. The winner is determined as follows: Rock wins over scissors (it crushes scissors), scissors wins over paper (it cuts paper), and paper wins over rock (it covers a rock).
4. The losing player then dribbles a ball to the other side of the room and back while the winner jumps up and down and says: "Ha, Ha. Ha, Ha."

Tips and Variations

- If dribbling the ball is too difficult, have players roll the ball.
- If dribbling the ball is too easy, have players dribble two balls.

Wall Passes

Objective

For two players to see how many consecutive passes they can make in a set amount of time

Equipment

- One stability ball per pair of players
- One chair (or a pair of cones) per pair of players
- A wall

Number of Players

Any number of pairs

Setup

- Two players lie on their backs beside each other, separated by a chair (or two cones).
- The players' legs are pointing up and leaning against the wall.
- One of the players has a stability ball resting on the soles of her feet and the wall.

Instructions

1. The person with the ball passes it up against the wall to her partner, who catches the ball between the bottoms of her feet and the wall.
2. Players continue passing the ball back and forth to each other and try to get as many successful consecutive passes as they can within a set amount of time, such as two minutes.
3. When the consecutive passes are broken, the players begin counting again from zero.

Tips and Variations

Wall Pass for Distance: Players see how far apart they can position themselves and still complete successful consecutive passes.

Seated Bounces

Objective

For two players to see how many consecutive bounce passes they can make in a set amount of time

Equipment

Three stability balls per pair of players

Number of Players

Any number of pairs

Setup

- One player leans against a ball that is between him and the wall. This player sits with his feet on the floor and knees bent at a 90-degree angle to the floor. Tell players to keep their knees behind their feet.
- The other player sits on a stability ball opposite the first player approximately 3 to 4 yards or meters away. This player holds another stability ball.

Instructions

1. On your signal to begin, players begin passing the ball back and forth to one other using one bounce and counting each catch.
2. Pairs try to get as many catches as they can in the set amount of time.
3. Players switch positions and try again.

Tips and Variations

- Distant Seated Bounces: Played the same as Seated Bounces except that players are farther apart and use a larger ball. You could also make two bounces mandatory for each throw.
- No-Bounce Seats: Played the same as Seated Bounces except that players cannot let the ball hit the floor.

Toss in the Towel

Objective

For two pairs of players to see how many consecutive passes they can make in a set amount of time

Equipment

- One stability ball for every four players
- Two towels for every four players

Number of Players

Groups of four

Setup

- Partners face each other holding a towel between them.
- One pair of partners (holding a ball between them in addition to their towel) stands beside another pair, approximately 3 to 4 yards or meters apart.

Instructions

1. On your signal to begin, the pair with the ball flips it into the other pair's towel.
2. Groups count the most consecutive passes they can make in the predetermined time limit (two minutes is usually a good time limit).

Tips and Variations

- Toss in the Towel for Distance: Once players succeed at the first pass, the passers take one sideways step away from the other set of partners, thereby increasing the distance of the next pass. If the next pass is successful, the passers take one sideways step away from the other set of partners. Pairs of players continue to move a step farther and farther apart in an effort to get as far apart as possible. However, if a ball hits the floor or ceiling, the players must move back and start from the beginning (or take one step closer together).
- Use a BOSU Ballast Ball to make this activity even more challenging.

Balancing Act

Objective

For two players to see how many different ways they can balance themselves on two stability balls

Equipment

One stability ball per player

Number of Players

Any number of pairs

Setup

- Players partner up.
- Each player has one stability ball.

Instructions

1. Instruct players to discover as many different ways as possible to balance on their own balls and be in contact with either their partners or their partners' balls.
2. Players must hold each balance for at least 10 seconds.

Tips and Variations

- For safety reasons, players should not be permitted to kneel or stand on their balls.
- One-Ball Balancing Act: Played the same as Balancing Act except two players balance on one ball.

Consecutive One-Bounce Passes

Objective

For two players to make as many consecutive one-bounce passes to each other as they can in one minute

Equipment

One stability ball per pair of players

Number of Players

Any number of pairs

Setup

- Two players sit opposite each other on the ground approximately 3 yards or meters apart.
- One player holds a stability ball.

Instructions

1. On your signal to begin, players pass the ball to each other as many times as possible in one minute.
2. The ball must bounce exactly once between players.
3. Each consecutive caught pass counts as one.
4. The winning pair is the pair that has the most consecutive caught passes in one minute.

Tips and Variations

- Move players farther apart and have them complete two-bounce passes each time.
- Standing One-Bounce Passes: Players stand facing each other, each with a ball in hand. On your signal to start, pairs try to complete as many passes as possible in the set amount of time.
- Use a BOSU Ballast Ball and try to pass the ball in the air with the filling not moving. Then, try to pass it with the ball spinning.

2

Races

There's nothing like a little competition between individuals or small teams to encourage them to pick up the pace and race to victory. The fastest way to complete some of these challenges is not always to go as fast as possible, but rather to compete in a controlled manner to achieve victory. For the highly active races, be sure to add a small break between games before repeating the fun or trying a new game.

World Cup Race

Objective

To be the quickest team to carry the World Cup trophy around the "stadium"

Equipment

- One extra-large stability ball per team
- Four cones

Number of Players

Teams of two to five players

Setup

- Put four cones toward the side of the playing area to create a large, square "stadium" around which the teams will race.

- Assign each team a starting cone and position the teams at their cone.
- Each team holds an extra-large stability ball above their heads, and each player is in contact with the ball with only one arm and hand.

Instructions

1. On your signal to begin, the teams carry their balls above their heads around the entire stadium while repeatedly singing the line "We are the champions."
2. If a team drops the ball, they must pick it up, run to the starting cone, and begin again.
3. When a team goes past the starting cone, they move to the inside and quietly pose for a "team picture."
4. The first team to complete the task is the champion.

Tips and Variations

- Players need to travel as a team and be careful not to trip on each other's feet.
- By having each player hold a short pool noodle, the team can carry the ball on top of the pool noodles and keep their feet farther from each other.

Twin Races

Objective

For a pair of runners to complete a race as quickly as possible

Equipment

One stability ball per pair

Number of Players

Any number of pairs

Setup

Establish a starting line and a finish line. These lines could be near each end of the room, or the route could constitute a lap around the room (going around the room is more difficult because players have to go around each other to pass).

Instructions

1. Each pair of players must carry a ball between them from the start of the race to the end. If they drop the ball, they must return to the starting line and begin again.
2. Here are some ways of holding the ball:
   - Players both hold a ball with both hands.
   - Players squeeze a ball together between their backs.
   - Players squeeze a ball together between their hips (no hands allowed on the ball).
   - Players squeeze a ball together between their knees (no hands allowed on the ball).

Tips and Variations

Triple Races: Played the same as Twin Races except that it is done in groups of three (or more).

Wall Bounce

Objective

For a team to count how many times it can bounce a ball against a wall in a specific amount of time

Equipment

One stability ball per team

Number of Players

Teams of two to four players

Setup

- Establish a throwing line approximately two to three paces from a wall. No one can pass a ball from in front of this line.
- Teams line up behind the throwing line with the front player in each line holding a stability ball.

Instructions

1. On your signal to begin, the first player of each team throws the ball against the wall. The first player then goes to the back of the team's line.
2. The second player in line stays behind the throwing line, catches the ball (which may or may not bounce on the floor), throws it at the wall, and then goes to the back of the line.
3. Players continue catching and throwing the ball, all the while counting the number of times the ball hits the wall, until you call out, "Stop."
4. The team with the most wall touches wins.

Tips and Variations

- You could specify that the ball has to bounce once before or after it hits the wall.
- Double Wall Bounce: Played the same as Wall Bounce except that the teams have two lines and two balls. The front players from each line pass the ball to the next person in the other line.

Carry the Crown

Objective

For pairs of players to carry a crown to safety as quickly as possible

Equipment

- One stability ball per pair of players
- One towel per pair of players

Number of Players

Any number of pairs

Setup

- Establish a starting line and a finish line. These lines could be near each end of the room, or the route could constitute a lap around the room (going around the room is more difficult because players have to go around each other to pass).
- Pairs of players (guards) line up at the starting line holding a towel between them. On the towel rests a stability ball (crown).

Instructions

On your signal to begin, the guards carry their crowns from the start of the race to the end. If they drop the crown, they must return to the starting line and begin again.

Tips and Variations

- Carry the Crowns to the Castle: Develop an obstacle course through which the players must travel, such as around chairs, under a pool noodle resting on the backs of two chairs, and so on.
- Have players use two pool noodles instead of a towel to carry the crown.

Crazy-Eights Dribble

Objective

To complete five laps of the figure-eight course as quickly as possible

Equipment

- One stability ball per player
- Two cones per game

Number of Players

Five to 10 players per game (or more if you make a larger course)

Setup

- Place two cones approximately 10 paces apart.
- All players hold stability balls in their hands and line up at one of the cones, facing the other cone.

Instructions

1. On your signal to begin, all the players dribble their balls, with their hands, around the left side of the first cone.
2. Players must go around the right side of the first cone and then around the left side of the second cone, completing figure eights.
3. Players complete five laps of the figure eight.

Tips and Variations

- With this many balls and players crossing through the middle of the figure eight at the same time, this is a game of considerable chaos. Encourage the players to enjoy the game and not to be too competitive.
- Make this race a relay race by having two or more teams on their own courses, with each team completing the course three or more times.
- Crazy-Eights Soccer: Played the same as Crazy-Eights Dribble except that players may use only their feet to advance the ball.
- Guarded Crazy Eights: Played the same as Crazy-Eights Dribble except that players may hit each other's balls away while bouncing their own.

Football

Objective

To pass a stability ball, using feet only, around the team as many times as possible in one minute

Equipment

One stability ball per team

Number of Players

Teams of four to six players

Setup

- Players lie on their backs in a circle with their heads in the middle and their feet pointing out.
- One player holds the ball between her feet.

Instructions

1. On your signal to begin, the player with the ball passes it to the player on her right.
2. Players may contact the ball only with their feet (no hands).
3. If any player touches the ball with her hands, or the ball falls out of the feet of a player, then the team begins counting consecutive passes anew.

Tips and Variations

Two-Ball Football: Give each team two balls to pass around.

Bounce and Follow

Objective

To make 15 passes as quickly as possible

Equipment

- One stability ball per team
- Two cones per team

Number of Players

Teams of three players

Setup

- Position two cones 4 to 5 yards or meters apart.
- One player stands to the left of one cone.
- The other two players stand one behind the other to the right of the opposite cone facing the single player. The player in the front holds the ball.

Instructions

1. On your signal to begin, the player with the ball bounces it to the player facing her.
2. Once the first player has passed the ball, she runs around the cone beside the player receiving the pass and then gets ready to receive a pass.
3. The player who received the pass catches the ball and bounces it to the player opposite her, and then follows the pass by running around the cone beside the player receiving the pass and gets ready to receive a pass.
4. Encourage players to call out the number for each pass received.
5. Once all players have received 15 passes, they repeatedly sing the line, "We are the champions!"

Tips and Variations

Have players use specific types of passes, kicks, or rolls to get the ball to the opposite player.

Mercury, Venus, Earth, and Mars

Objective

To be the quickest player to circumnavigate the sun within the orbits of Mercury, Venus, Earth, and Mars

Equipment

- One stability ball per player
- 16 cones

Number of Players

Depends on the size of the solar system, but four to six players at a time is ideal

Setup

- Choose a spot in the middle of the floor to be the sun.
- Approximately two paces from the sun, place four cones identifying Mercury's orbit.
- Approximately two more paces from Mercury's orbit, place four cones identifying Venus' orbit, and do the same for the orbits of Earth and Mars.
- Place a starting line about six paces from the first cone of Mars. All players line up at the starting line with their balls in front of them.

Instructions

1. On your signal to begin, all the players leave at the same time (and fun meteoric chaos results) and shove, kick, or dribble (you need to specify the type of ball movement) their balls toward Mars' orbit, where they must do a complete rotation. They then do a complete rotation of Earth's orbit, then Venus,' and then Mercury's, at which point they bring the ball to the sun.
2. The first player to get his ball to the sun is the winner.

Tips and Variations

None

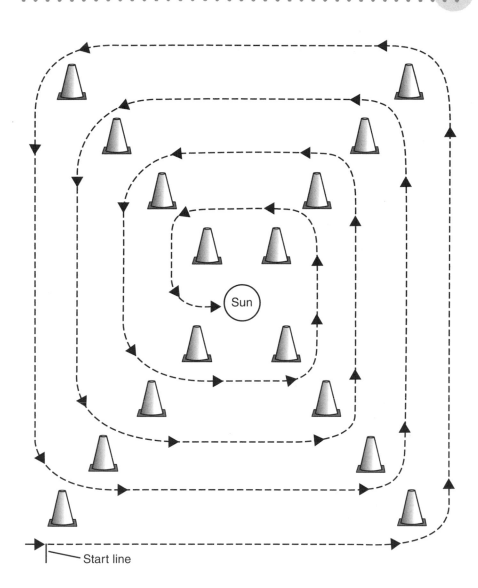

Start line

Pass, Floor, Pass

Objective

For two players to pass the ball and touch it to the ground as many consecutive times as possible in a set amount of time

Equipment

One stability ball per pair

Number of Players

Any number of pairs

Setup

- Two players lie beside each other with their heads in opposite directions.
- One player holds the ball on the ground between his legs.

Instructions

1. On your signal to begin, the player with the ball lifts it up with his legs and passes it to his partner's lifted legs.
2. When the partner receives the ball, he touches it to the ground and brings it back up to pass it back to his partner in the same manner.
3. Players count the number of times the ball touches the ground in two minutes.

Tips and Variations

Decrease or increase the time depending on the strength and abilities of your players.

Running Triangles

Objective

For each pair to pass and run around the triangle as quickly as possible

Equipment

- One stability ball per pair
- Three cones per pair

Number of Players

Any number of pairs

Setup

- Place three cones 5 to 10 yards or meters apart in a triangle shape.
- Players position themselves at two of the corners of the triangle.
- One player holds the ball.

Instructions

1. On your signal to begin, the player with the ball throws it to the other player and then runs to the open cone.
2. The player who receives the ball throws it to the other player, who should be at the new cone. The player who threw the ball then runs to the new open cone.
3. Passes continue until the first passer has returned to the starting cone a fourth time.
4. The first pair to finish wins.

Tips and Variations

- Increase the activity of this game by increasing the laps required, the distance between the cones, or both.
- Decrease the activity of this game by having four players per triangle with two players at one cone. The ball begins where there are two players at a cone. The player who throws the ball follows the ball to the cone he threw it at and replaces the player who caught and threw the ball to the next cone.
- Have players use different throws or rolls to pass the ball.

3

Relays

In relays, players in small teams encourage each other to accomplish the team's goals. Relays can involve very quick games of bouncing balls against a wall to slower but more demanding games, such as a crab walk. To ensure that all players remain active, make sure teams are no larger than four players. Otherwise, players spend too much time waiting around, become bored, and are not active. If the relays involve finish lines, be sure to keep the finish lines a safe distance from end walls.

Crab Walk Relay

Objective

To be the quickest team to accomplish a crab walk with the stability ball

Equipment

- One stability ball per team
- One cone per team

Number of Players

Teams of three or four players

Setup

- Establish a starting line and place a cone two paces from the starting line.
- Have teams stand behind the starting line.
- The front player is in a "crab walk" position, with her hands on the starting line, her back toward the cone, and her feet on the ball, waiting for the start of the relay.
- To crab walk, a player sits on the floor and puts the back of her heels and calves on her ball and her hands on the floor. To move, she must lift up her buttocks, walk backward with her hands, and move her feet to keep them on top of the ball. This activity is excellent for strengthening arms, shoulders, abdomen, and legs.

Instructions

1. On your signal to begin, the first player in line crab walks her ball around the cone and back to the starting line.
2. When she touches the starting line with her hands, she stands up, picks up the ball, and places it under the feet of the second racer, who has her hands on the starting line and her back facing the cone, ready to race.
3. The second player races around the cone and back.
4. While the racers are on their way toward the cone and back, the rest of the players on the team do slow-speed jumping jacks and cheer their players on.
5. When the entire team has completed the race, the team sits down.
6. The team that completes the race and is seated first is the winner.

Tips and Variations

- Adjust the distance from the starting line to the cone according to the overall ability of the group to do the crab walk.
- Crab Walk Balance: Played the same as Crab Walk Relay except that the players' feet are also on the ground and the ball is balanced on top of their bellies.

Over, Under, and Around Relay

Objective

To be the quickest team to move a stability ball over, under, and around the body of each team member twice

Equipment

One stability ball per team

Number of Players

Teams of three to five players

Setup

Each team stands around its stability ball, which is on the ground.

Instructions

1. Give the teams two minutes to determine the quickest way to get the stability ball completely over, under, and around the body of each team member.

2. On your signal to begin, each team moves the ball over, under, and around each team member.

3. When the team has completed the challenge twice, the team members sit in a line behind the ball and cheer.

4. The first team to complete the task is the winner.

Tips and Variations

Try other types of movement patterns, such as over, a different over, and under; or under, a different under, and over.

Target Relay

Objective

To get the stability ball to rest on an inner tube or ball stand as many times as possible in a set amount of time

Equipment

- One stability ball per team
- One inner tube or ball stand per team

Number of Players

Teams of three to five players

Setup

- Have teams line up behind a starting or tossing line.
- Place an inner tube or ball stand for each team about three to five paces from the starting or tossing line.
- The first player in line holds the stability ball.

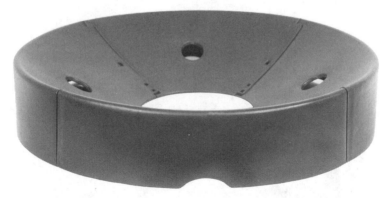

Reprinted, by permission, from Power Systems. Available: www.resistaball.com

Instructions

1. On your signal to begin, the first player in line throws, bounces, or rolls the ball to try to get it to balance on top of the inner tube or ball stand. This scores one point.
2. Regardless of success, the first player retrieves the ball, passes it to the second player in line, and goes to the back of the team's line.
3. After a set amount of time, call, "Stop." The team with the most points wins.

Tips and Variations

You might have an easier time obtaining old tires than inner tubes, although they are heavier and more difficult to move around.

Circle Relay

Objective

To be the first team to have everyone circle the team

Equipment

One stability ball per team

Number of Players

Teams of four to six players

Setup

- Each team stands in a tight circle with a stability ball in the middle.
- Number players in each team consecutively one, two, three, and so on, in a clockwise direction.

Instructions

1. On your signal to begin, the first player from each team pulls the ball out of the middle of the circle and rolls it on the floor around the circle in a clockwise direction. When the first player has completed the circle, the number two player takes the ball and rolls it around the circle.

2. Each player takes a turn to complete a circle.

3. When the last player of the team has completed the circle, the team members pick the ball up together and hold it above their heads, repeatedly singing, "We are the champions!"

Tips and Variations

- Encourage the other team members to jump up and down and cheer for the player going around the circle.
- Soccer Circle Relay: Played the same as Circle Relay except that players use their feet and legs to move the ball around the circle.
- Bounce Circle Relay: Played the same as Circle Relay except that players bounce the ball as they move it around the circle.

Dribble Relay

Objective

To be the quickest team to have each player dribble a ball around an obstacle course

Equipment

- One stability ball per team
- Four cones per team

Number of Players

Teams of three or four players

Setup

- Set up a similar obstacle course for each team, using the four cones.
- Teams line up behind a starting line with the first player in line holding the stability ball.

Instructions

1. On your signal to begin, the first player in each team dribbles (bounces) the ball around the team's cones.
2. When the first player comes back to the starting line, she gives the ball to the second player, who completes the obstacle course. The same process occurs for the remaining players.
3. While the players are dribbling their balls around the cones, the rest of the team does jumping jacks as they cheer the dribblers on.
4. When the final player crosses the starting line, the first player takes the ball again, and the team sits quietly in a line behind the first player. The first team to complete the obstacle and sit down is the winner.

Tips and Variations

- Soccer Dribble Relay: Played the same as Dribble Relay except that players must dribble the ball using only their feet and legs.
- Shuffle Dribble Relay: Played the same as Dribble Relay except that players must place the balls of their feet on two pieces of carpet (if the course is on carpet, use two pieces of scrap paper) and shuffle around the obstacle course while dribbling the ball with their hands.

Pass Relay

Objective

For three players to count how many passing laps they can complete in a set amount of time

Equipment

One stability ball per three players

Number of Players

Any number of threesomes

Setup

- Players stand in a line a predetermined distance apart (three to five paces works well).
- A player at the end of the line holds the ball.

Instructions

1. On your signal to begin, the first player passes the ball to the middle player, who passes the ball to the player at the other end of the line. The player at the other end of the line passes the ball back to the player in the middle, who passes it back to the first player. This counts as one lap.
2. On your signal to stop, players determine how many laps they made.
3. Players repeat the relay.

Tips and Variations

- Round the Triangle Pass Relay: Played the same as Pass Relay except that players stand in a triangle formation and pass the ball around the triangle as many times as possible in the time established. You could specify different types of passes to use in each game.
- Use a BOSU Ballast Ball to make these relays more challenging.

Sweeper Relay

Objective

To be the quickest team to complete the race

Equipment

- One towel per team
- One stability ball per team

Number of Players

Teams of three or four players

Setup

- Have teams line up behind a starting line with a towel and a ball lying in front of the first player in line.
- Set up a cone in front of each team, approximately 5 to 10 paces from the starting line.
- Keep starting lines and turning cones well away from any walls.

Instructions

1. On your signal to begin, the first player of each team puts both hands on the towel and pushes the stability ball with his head around the cone and back to the starting line.
2. When the first player crosses the starting line, he gives the ball to the second player, who completes the obstacle course. The same process occurs for the remaining players.
3. While the players are pushing their balls around the cones, the rest of the team members do a cleaning-the-window action with their hands as they cheer their sweepers on.
4. When the final player crosses the starting line, he gives the ball to the first player again, and the team sits quietly in a line behind the first player.
5. The team that finishes the relay and sits down first wins.

Tips and Variations

To reduce wait times for the players and to make the pushing position easier, shorten the course and have the teams go through the course twice.

Wall Roll Relay

Objective

To pass a stability ball along a wall as quickly as possible

Equipment

One stability ball per team

Number of Players

Teams of three to five players

Setup

- Determine the distances the teams need to cover.
- Have players lie beside each other on their backs with their feet up and leaning against a wall.
- The first person in the line balances a ball on her feet and the wall.

Instructions

1. On your signal to begin, the first player rolls the ball to rest on the feet of the next player in line.
2. The first person then runs to the end of the line and prepares to receive the ball.
3. If the ball falls or if players touch it with their hands, the whole team must begin again.
4. The first team to finish is the winner.

Tips and Variations

Two-Ball Wall Roll: With a larger group, use two balls at the same time, with players getting up and running to the ends of the lines once they have passed the second ball.

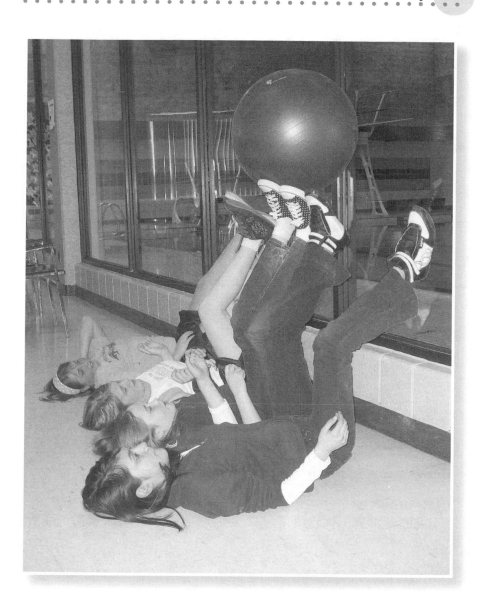

Le Mans 24-Lap Relay

Objective

To be the quickest team to roll a ball around a square course

Equipment

- One stability ball per team
- Four cones per game

Number of Players

Teams of two or three players

Setup

- With the cones, mark a square 5 to 10 yards or meters across. The more teams there are, the larger the square should be.
- Have each team pick an exchange spot on the track and stand inside the square at that location.
- One player from each team stands on the track at the team's exchange spot with a ball in front of him.

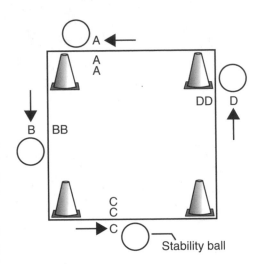
Stability ball

Instructions

1. On your signal to begin, the player with the ball rolls the ball once around the square.
2. When the player returns to the exchange area, his teammate runs a lap with the ball while the first pusher takes a brief break inside the exchange area. When the second player returns to the exchange area, the third teammate runs a lap with the ball while the first and second pushers take a brief break inside the exchange area.
3. The first team to complete 24 laps is the victor.

Tips and Variations

- Have the teams do the race again but in the opposite direction.
- Instead of having the players roll the ball, have them dribble it or kick it around the track.

4

Tag Games

Everyone loves a game of tag. It is often as much fun to be chased as it is to be "It" (the chaser). Be sure, though, that the Its do not stay It unduly long, or they will tire and become frustrated. Playing tag while sitting on, passing, or dribbling a stability ball adds hilarious and challenging twists to traditional games of tag in which players simply run around.

Last One Tagged It

Objective

To be the last player tagged

Equipment

One stability ball per player

Number of Players

Any number of players

Setup

- Assign boundaries for the game. Half a volleyball court is approximately 9 paces by 9 paces, or 81 square paces—enough room for about 16 players.
- Players sit on balls scattered around the playing area.
- Assign one player to be the It.

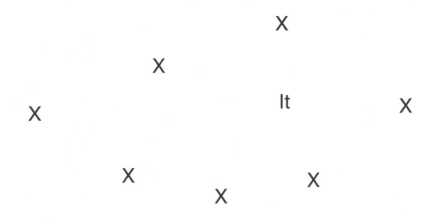

Instructions

1. On your signal to begin, the players use a forward roll to move inside the playing area in an effort to avoid being tagged by the It. To forward roll, players sit on their balls and then roll forward until they almost fall off the front of their balls. Players then squat up and pull their balls under their bottoms again to a sitting position. Players roll forward again and repeat as they move around the playing surface.
2. The It tries to tag players.
3. When the It tags a player, then there are two Its.
4. If a player goes out of bounds, that player also becomes an It.
5. The game continues until only one player remains untagged. That player is the winner and becomes the It for the next game.

Tips and Variations

- If the player who is It is not quick enough to tag other players, suggest that she try to corner players and then tag them.
- Do not allow players to move backward on their balls; doing so risks falling backward and hitting the backs of their heads on the floor.
- This is an excellent game for strengthening the upper legs and shoulders.

Pursuit Tag

Objective

To switch from the outside circle to the inside circle and back to the outside circle as few times as possible

Equipment

- One stability ball per player
- Eight cones

Number of Players

Five to 20 players

Setup

- Place one set of four cones in a square with approximately 10 paces between cones, and set up another square of cones inside this outer square approximately five paces apart.
- Have players position themselves outside the outer four cones and place their stability balls in front of them.

Instructions

1. On your signal to begin, players run counterclockwise around the outside of the square created by the outside four cones, while pushing their stability balls.
2. Players try to tag the balls of the players in front of them. When this happens, the tagged player moves to the inside circle. As more players arrive in the inside circle, they move counterclockwise and try to tag the balls of the players in front of them. Players tagged in the inside circle rejoin the outside circle.
3. After a set amount of time, call out, "Stop." At that point, players count the number of times they moved from the outside circle to the inside circle and vice versa. The player who moved the fewest times is the winner.

Tips and Variations

- Pool Noodle Pursuit Tag: Played the same as Pursuit Tag except that players propel their balls forward with one hand and hold a long pool noodle in the other. When they touch the players in front of them with the pool noodle, the front players move into the other circle.
- Two-Player Pursuit: Played the same as Pursuit Tag except that you place one set of cones in a square with approximately 3 paces between cones. Players start at opposite corners of the square. On your signal to begin, each player runs counterclockwise around the cones and tries to tag the player in front of him. When he succeeds, the tagged person goes into the middle of the square and a third person enters opposite the winner. The tagging process then begins again, with the tagged person taking a break until the next person is tagged.

Ball Safe

Objective

To avoid being tagged by the It

Equipment

- Three stability balls per 10 players
- One pool noodle per 10 players

Number of Players

Any number of players

Setup

- Players are in a scattered position.
- Assign one It per 10 players and give each of the Its a pool noodle to tag the other players with.
- Scatter the stability balls around the playing area.

Instructions

1. On your signal to begin, players run around trying to avoid being tagged by the Its.
2. One way to be safe is to be in contact with a stability ball. Players can help each other by rolling or tossing a ball to a player in danger of being tagged.
3. When a second player touches the ball, the first player must let go of the ball.
4. When a player is tagged, he does jumping jacks in one spot until another player rolls a ball to him.
5. After the tagged player touches a ball that another player has rolled to him, he can resume normal play again.

Tips and Variations

Foot and Leg Ball Safe: Played the same as Ball Safe except that the only way players can touch or move a ball is with a leg or foot.

Island Tag

Objective

To avoid getting tagged by one's partner

Equipment

One stability ball per player

Number of Players

Any number of players

Setup

- Each player stands beside a stability ball and puts one hand on top of it.
- Players choose partners.
- Determine playing boundaries to keep all players in a fairly confined space (30 players on half a volleyball court [9 square yards or meters] or smaller).

Instructions

1. Have partners play a game of Rock, Paper, Scissors to determine who is It.
2. On your signal, the Its hold onto their balls and walk around them twice to give their partners an opportunity to move away.
3. Players move around the playing area by rolling their ball around.
4. When the It is successful in tagging her partner, her partner is the new It and walks around her ball twice and then tries to tag her partner.

Tips and Variations

- Island Dribble Tag: Played the same as Island Tag except that the players bounce their balls as they move around the island.
- The more confined the area is and the more players you have, the better.

Frozen Tag

Objective

To avoid getting tagged by the It

Equipment

- One stability ball per 20 players
- One pool noodle for each It

Number of Players

Any number of players

Setup

- Players are in a scattered position in the playing area.
- Place one stability ball in the middle of the playing area.
- Designate one or more players to be It, and give them each a pool noodle with which to tag the other players.

Instructions

1. On your signal to begin, the Its run around and tag other players with their pool noodles.
2. If a player is tagged, both of his feet are frozen to the ground.
3. If another player hits the frozen player with the ball, the frozen player is automatically thawed out and can resume normal play.
4. When all players are frozen, the It wins.

Tips and Variations

If the Its are having trouble freezing all the players, add more Its or replace the Its frequently.

Dribble Tag

Objective

To avoid being tagged by the It

Equipment

- One stability ball per player
- One pool noodle for the It

Number of Players

Any number of players

Setup

- All players start inside a defined playing area holding a ball.
- Assign one player to be the It (add more Its if there are a lot of players), and give the It a pool noodle.

Instructions

1. On your signal to begin, everyone, including the It, dribbles a ball in the designated area. The It tries to tag players with the pool noodle she is holding in her other hand.
2. When a player is tagged, goes out of bounds, or loses her ball, she gets the pool noodle and becomes the new It.

Tips and Variations

Dribble Ball Tag: Played the same as Dribble Tag except that the It must hit another player's ball with the pool noodle for that player to become the new It.

Pressure Tag

Objective

To avoid being tagged by an It

Equipment

- One stability ball per pair of players
- Two pool noodles per pair of Its

Number of Players

Any number of players

Setup

- Players select partners and with their partners are scattered around the playing area.
- Partners squeeze their stability balls between their bodies; they may not hold the balls up with their hands or arms while moving.
- One pair of players for every five to seven pairs is assigned to be the It, and that pair is given two pool noodles with which to tag other players.

Instructions

1. On your signal to begin, the Its try to tag other players. When they succeed, or when chased players drop their balls, the Its give them their pool noodles and they become the new Its.
2. If the ball starts to fall, partners can stop briefly, place the ball higher with their hands, and then move again without touching the ball with their hands. No moving is allowed while holding the ball with the hands.

Tips and Variations

Trio Pressure Tag: Played the same as Pressure Tag except that three (or more) players squeeze a ball among them as they move about the playing area.

All It

Objective

To tag others while not getting tagged

Equipment

One small stability ball per player

Number of Players

Any number of players

Setup

Players are scattered throughout the playing area sitting on small stability balls.

Instructions

1. On your signal to begin, players move around the playing area by bouncing around while remaining seated on their stability balls.
2. Each time a player touches someone else's ball with any part of his body, he scores a point. Players should call out their total points after each tag.
3. A player cannot tag the same ball twice, nor can the person just tagged tag the ball of the person that just tagged him without first tagging someone else's ball.

Tips and Variations

It is more challenging to have to tag other players, not just their balls. If two players tag each other simultaneously, they play a game of Rock, Paper, Scissors. The winner scores the point.

Ball Tag

Objective

For a pair of Its to tag another player with the ball

Equipment

One extra-small stability ball per game

Number of Players

Ten to 15 players per game

Setup

- Establish a small playing area (a 6-yard or 6-meter square works well).
- All players are inside the playing area.
- Designate two players to be Its, and give one of them a stability ball.

Instructions

1. On your signal to begin, the Its pass the ball to each other and try to tag someone by touching them with the ball.
2. The It without the ball can move around the square to get in position to catch the ball and tag a player with it.
3. The It with the ball can pivot on one foot only.
4. Tagged players or those who go out of bounds switch roles with the It with the ball.

Tips and Variations

- Tactically, it is advantageous for the Its to make quick, short passes as they try to corner a player.
- If you have a larger area, have three Its or two pairs of players be Its, each with a ball. The two pairs can work independently or cooperate in catching other players.

5

Group Games

Competing in larger groups is socially rewarding. The activities in this chapter range from individuals leading the rest of the group in exercises to trying not to get caught in a game of Bulldog. There are plenty of opportunities for individuals to shine as they explore various ways to throw and catch stability balls.

Help

Objective

For players in the corners of the playing area not to be tagged or to have their passes intercepted by the "thief"

Equipment

- One stability ball per group
- Four cones per group

Number of Players

Four players per game

Setup

- Put four cones in a square shape approximately six paces apart.
- Designate one player to stand in the middle of the square; this player is the "thief."
- One player stands at one of the cones with the ball in hand.
- The other two players stand by the cones adjacent to the player with the ball.

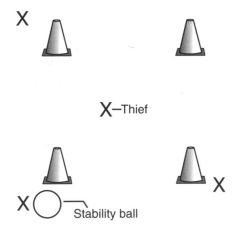

Instructions

1. When everyone is ready, play begins with the thief trying to tag the player with the ball or intercept the pass.

2. The player with the ball passes it to one of the other two players. When the new player has the ball, the player who did not get the ball runs to the empty corner so that the thrower has two options to pass to. A thrower can throw the ball only to the player at the cone immediately to the left or right; he cannot pass across the square.

Tips and Variations

You may specify that all passes need to be in the air, or need to be bounce passes.

Four Square (King's Court)

Objective

To stay in the king's court

Equipment

One stability ball

Number of Players

Four to seven players

Setup

- Make a four-square box (4 yards or meters in diameter and divided into four squares).
- Define one small square as the king's square, and number the other squares 3, 2, and 1.
- Choose four players to stand in the four squares; the extra players wait outside square 1.

King	3
1	2

Extra players ➡ XXX

Instructions

1. The king has the ball, bounces it off the ground, and then hits it into one of the other squares. The hit ball must bounce in a neighboring square (bouncing on the lines of a square counts as being in the square).
2. The player whose square the ball lands in must hit the ball in an upward trajectory so that it lands in one of the neighboring squares.
3. If a player fails to hit the ball into a neighboring square, that player is eliminated. The eliminated player goes to the back of the extra players' line.
4. When a player is eliminated, all other players move up to fill that spot. For example, if the eliminated player is in square 1, the next extra player moves into that square. If the eliminated player is in square 2, the player in square 1 moves into square 2 and an extra player moves into square 1. If the eliminated player is in square 3, the player in square 2 moves into square 3, the player in square 1 moves into square 2, and an extra player moves into square 1. If the king is eliminated, everyone moves up one square and the new player moves into square 1.

Tips and Variations

The players who are waiting can remain active by jogging slowly, or doing another activity that you specify, well outside the big square so they do not get in the way of the other players.

Clear the Deck

Objective

To be the player who left the deck the fewest number of times

Equipment

One stability ball per player

Number of Players

Any number of players

Setup

- Assign boundaries that are at least 5 square yards or meters per player (half a volleyball court is 9 meters wide, or 81 square meters, which is enough room for about 16 players).
- Players are scattered around the playing area touching their stability balls with only one hand (no two-handed holding or sitting on the balls).
- All players are It.

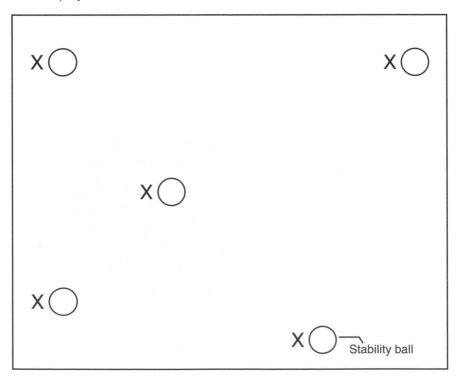

Stability ball

Instructions

1. On your signal to begin, players move around the playing area and try to hit (with their hands) other players' stability balls outside the boundaries of the playing area.

2. If a player's stability ball goes outside the playing area, she may retrieve it, carry it back into the center of the playing area, and resume play.

3. At the end of the time limit (three to five minutes should be sufficient), ask players how many times they each went outside the playing area; the ones who went out the fewest number of times win.

Tips and Variations

If there are two courts, players who are knocked out of one court go to the second court. Players who are knocked out of the second court resume play in the first court. Players try to move from court to court the fewest number of times.

Ball Is in Your Court

Objective

For various people to lead the group in a variety of exercises on the stability ball

Equipment

- One stability ball per player
- One tennis ball per group

Number of Players

Any number of players

Setup

Players are in a circle facing in so they can see each other.

Instructions

1. Give a tennis ball to one of the players.
2. The player with the tennis ball leads the group in a specific exercise on the stability ball. A list of exercises can be found in the Tips and Variations section of this game.
3. When the player with the tennis ball has decided the activity is over, she passes the tennis ball to another player. Or, if the other players think they have done the exercise long enough, they call out, "Pass the ball," and the player with the tennis ball must pass it to another player.
4. The group continues with the exercise they are engaged in until a new leader with the tennis ball begins a new exercise. The group then follows the new leader in doing the new exercise.

Tips and Variations

All of the following exercises can be found in Lorne Goldenberg and Peter Twist's book *Strength Ball Training, Second Edition,* published in 2007 by Human Kinetics (Champaign, IL), on the page numbers listed after the activity name.

- Triceps Blaster (page 237)—Players lean on their balls with their forearms and do push-ups. Their bodies are straight. Refer to number 3 in the Instructions section until someone says, "Pass the ball."

- Ball Walk-Around (pages 170-171)—Players are in push-up positions with their feet on the tops of their balls. They then walk with their hands one lap around their balls.
- Jackknife (pages 26-27)—Players are in push-up positions with their feet on the tops of their balls. They then pull their balls toward them so that their heels almost touch their buttocks.
- Balance Push-Up (pages 46-47)—Players start in push-up positions on their balls with their hands on their balls and their bodies straight. Then they slowly bend their arms and drop their chests to the balls and then push back up again.
- Kneeling Rollout (pages 60-61)—Players kneel and place their balls slightly in front of them, placing their hands on the sides of the balls closest to their bodies. The players then rock forward on their knees and allow their balls to move away from them. Players keep their torsos straight and do not go too far so as to hyperextend their lower backs.
- Wrap Sit-Up (page 210-211)—Players place their feet flat on the floor and lie with their whole backs covering their balls. Then they pull their bodies up to 45-degree angles from their balls. Do not allow players to tuck their chins down.
- Abdominal Side Crunch (pages 214-215)—Players place their feet flat on the ground and lie with the sides of their bodies covering their balls, with their arms crossing their upper bodies. Then they lift their upper bodies until their knees, hips, and shoulders are all in line.

Stretch

Objective

To be the only one touching a stability ball as soon as the music stops

Equipment

- One stability ball for every two players
- CD player
- CD of slower music

Number of Players

Any number of players

Setup

Scatter the stability balls around the playing area.

Instructions

1. Play some music and specify the way the players should move, such as taking giant steps forward, taking giant steps backward, taking side steps, rolling like a log on the floor, crab walking, walking while swimming (front crawl, breaststroke, backstroke), walking and high-fiving a different person each time, or frog jumping.

2. When you stop the music, all players must continue the assigned movement pattern and touch a stability ball. Only one person can be touching each ball. If two people simultaneously claim a ball, they both run a lap.

3. Once all of the stability balls have been contacted, the remaining players do one (or more) slow jogs around the room. The players with the balls perform stretching activities with their balls.

4. Start the music again and specify a different movement pattern.

Tips and Variations

- All of the following stretching exercises can be found in Lorne Goldenberg and Peter Twist's book *Strength Ball Training, Second Edition,* published in 2007 by Human Kinetics (Champaign, IL).

  - Hip Extension and Knee Flexion (pages 110-111)—Players lie on their backs with their feet on the tops of their balls. Then they contract their abdominal muscles so their bodies are straight and bring their heels toward their buttocks.

- Spinal Extension (page 268)—Players lie on their balls so that the natural curves of their lower backs cover the balls. Then players push their balls toward their heads to fully stretch their backs.
- Lateral Side Stretch (page 269)—Players lie in a lateral position over their balls. Players may need to do this close to a wall so they can use the wall for stability.
- Standing Hamstring Stretch (page 271)—Players place one of their feet on top of their balls. Then they move their navels toward their thighs and stretch their hamstrings.
- This activity works well as a cool-down at the end of an active session.

Pass the Ball

Objective

For players to take turns leading an exercise

Equipment

- One stability ball per group
- CD player
- CD of lively music

Number of Players

Any number of players; groups of 10 to 15 players are ideal

Setup

- Players stand in a circle; one person has the stability ball.
- Play music.

Instructions

1. The player with the ball leads an exercise activity not involving the ball.
2. Someone from the group calls out, "Pass the ball!" When that call is made, the person with the ball passes it to another player in the group.
3. Players continue the exercises they were doing until the new person begins a new exercise, at which point everyone then does the new exercise.
4. Participants continue exercising and passing the ball to do new exercises.

Tips and Variations

- You could encourage slower activities at the beginning of the game, more vigorous ones in the middle few minutes of the game, and then stretches at the end of the game.
- You can control the speed of the exercises somewhat according to the energy level of the music.

Musical Balls

Objective

To be touching a stability ball as soon as the music stops

Equipment

- One stability ball for every two players
- CD player
- CD of lively music

Number of Players

Any number of players

Setup

Scatter the stability balls around the playing area.

Instructions

1. Play some music and specify the way the players should move, such as speed walking, galloping, hopping on one foot, hopping on two feet, lunge stepping, slow jogging with high knee lifts, slow jogging with feet contacting the buttocks, skier hopping, bunny hopping, or heel-to-toe walking.
2. When you stop the music, all players must continue the assigned movement pattern and touch a stability ball.
3. Remove one or more stability balls.
4. Start the music again, and have players perform a different movement pattern.
5. Continue the activity until only one ball is left and all the players are trying to touch the one ball.

Tips and Variations

This game is a great activity for clearing the balls from the floor and encouraging group solidarity.

Circus Toss and Catch

Objective

For players to discover as many ways as possible to toss a ball and catch it themselves

Equipment

One stability ball per player

Number of Players

Any number of players

Setup

Give each player a stability ball and position the players a safe distance from each other and any obstructions (at least three paces apart).

Instructions

1. On your signal to begin, the players discover and perform as many ways as they can to toss a ball and catch it themselves.
2. Have the players with the most original ways of tossing and catching demonstrate their techniques.

Tips and Variations

- You could add specific challenges, such as having players toss with their hands and catch with anything but their hands, or toss with any part of their bodies and catch with their hands.
- Have players bounce their balls off the floor and wall between tosses and catches to add even more variety.

Field Meet

Objective

To complete a field course with the best possible score

Equipment

- One 20-yard or 20-meter measuring tape for each throwing event and one 5-yard or 5-meter measuring tape for the high jump
- At least one small stability ball per station (the game is more active if there is one ball per two players; one player completes the activity while the other measures the distance)

Number of Players

Two to six players to a station

Setup

Set up the stations listed in the instructions.

Instructions

1. Shot Put: Players cradle stability balls on their shoulders and one hand. They propel the balls with their hand as far as they can. Measure where the balls land.
2. Triple Jump: From a stationary position, players toss their balls with two hands as far as possible. The distance is measured at the spot where the balls land on the third bounce.
3. Hammer Throw: Players stand backward to where they plan to throw their balls. They hold their balls and throw them over their heads as far as possible. The measurement is taken from where the balls first bounce.
4. High Jump: Players bounce their balls hard on the ground and try to get them to bounce as high as possible. Measure the approximate highest point that the balls go up to. If players are strong and their first bounce is too difficult to measure, measure the height of the second bounce.

Tips and Variations

- Increase the size of the ball to make the challenges more difficult.
- If the ball hits the ceiling, the throw doesn't count.
- To calculate an overall champion, add up the total distance for each event.

Rolling Bulldogs

Objective

To cross from one end of the court to the other without getting hit by a rolling stability ball

Equipment

One stability ball for every 10 players

Number of Players

Five to 30 players

Setup

- Define two lines that are at least four paces from the walls (to prevent players from falling into the wall if they trip after they cross the line).
- Choose one to four players to line up between the lines with stability balls in front of them.
- All the other players line up behind one of the lines.

Instructions

1. One of the players in the middle calls out, "Bulldog," at which point the other players try to run from one side of the court to the other.
2. The players in the middle try to roll the stability balls against the players crossing the court.
3. If a crossing player is touched by a ball, that player and the player who rolled the ball switch places.

Tips and Variations

- Survivor Rolling Bulldogs: Played the same as Rolling Bulldogs except that players touched by balls join the rollers in the middle and help them until there is only one player left; that player is the survivor, the winner.
- It is helpful to add an additional ball for every two players who go in the middle.

Parachute Roll

Objective

To get the ball to move as many times around the parachute as possible in a set amount of time

Equipment

- One stability ball per group
- One parachute per group

Number of Players

Ten to 20 players (or more if you have a larger parachute)

Setup

- Players stand around a parachute and hold it waist high.
- Place a ball on the parachute near one edge.

Instructions

1. On your signal to begin, players drop and lift the parachute to get the stability ball to roll around the parachute.
2. Each lap counts as one. The group tries to get as many successive laps as possible until time runs out.
3. If the ball falls off the parachute, the lap count goes back to zero.

Tips and Variations

Seated or Lying-Down Parachute Roll: Played the same as Parachute Roll except that players sit down with their legs under the parachute, or lie down under the parachute with only their heads sticking out; they hold the parachute up with straight arms.

6

Group Challenges

The games in this chapter require some leadership from the players to determine the best (and often the fastest) way to overcome group challenges. Many of these games involve passing the ball over, under, or around the group. Some involve innovative ways of passing the ball. For example, in Feet Pass, players can pass the ball only with their feet, and in Circular Moving Sidewalk, the players are lying down and can pass the ball only with outstretched hands.

Over the Top

Objective

To pass a stability ball overhead the most successive times in a set amount of time

Equipment

One stability ball per group

Number of Players

Groups of 4 to 10 players

Setup

- Players stand in a line with their groups, facing the backs of the players in front of them.
- Make sure there is enough distance behind the last player in line for someone to either go behind or stand to one side to have the group turn a corner if it gets too close to a wall.
- Give the front player the ball.

Instructions

1. On your signal to begin, the front player passes the ball overhead back to the second player in line. The front player then runs to the back of the line. Each player does the same after passing the ball back.
2. The ball is passed to the end of the line, at which point the first player is now at the back of the line behind the last player and the players continue to pass the ball back.
3. Have the groups count each successive time the ball goes past the first player.
4. If the ball falls to the ground, the counting begins anew. Groups should keep track of the highest number of successive passes through the group during the allotted time (one or two minutes should be adequate).

Tips and Variations

Forward Over the Top: Played the same as Over the Top except that players pass the ball forward instead of backward. This version is more challenging because the player in front cannot as easily see the ball coming (though they are permitted to look backward).

Over and Under

Objective

To pass a stability ball overhead and under the legs the most consecutive times in a set amount of time

Equipment

One stability ball per group

Number of Players

Groups of four to six players

Setup

- Players stand in a line with their groups, facing the backs of the players in front of them about one pace apart from each other.
- Make sure there is enough distance behind the last player in line for someone to either go behind or stand to one side to have the group turn a corner when it gets too close to a wall.
- Give the front player the ball.

Instructions

1. On your signal to begin, the front player passes the ball back overhead to the second player in line. The front player then runs to the back of the line.
2. The second player puts the ball down on the ground and passes it under his legs to the next player in line.
3. Players alternate between passing the ball overhead and passing it under the legs before running to the back of the line.
4. The ball is passed to the end of the line, at which point the first player is now at the back of the line behind the last player and the players continue to pass the ball back.
5. Have the groups count each successive time the ball goes past the first player.
6. Groups should keep track of the highest number of successive passes through the group during the allotted time (one or two minutes should be adequate).

Tips and Variations

- Forward Over and Under: Played the same as Over and Under except that players pass the ball forward instead of backward. This version is more challenging because the player in front cannot as easily see the ball coming (though they are permitted to look backward).
- Using a BOSU Ballast Ball will add balance and strength components to the game.

Jog Toss

Objective

To run around the playing area, tossing a ball and catching that of the player in front

Equipment

- One stability ball per player
- Four cones

Number of Players

Any number of players

Setup

- Determine an area that allows all the players to jog in a circle with three to four paces between them.
- Mark off the area with four cones.
- Players stand in a circle approximately three to four paces behind the players in front of them, facing counterclockwise. If the players are too close, then make the area larger. If the players are too far apart, make the area smaller. If you have too many players, make another area inside the first area.
- Give each player a stability ball.

Instructions

1. At your signal to begin, players jog around the designated area, carrying their stability balls.
2. When you call out, "Now!" the players toss their balls straight up into the air, but keep running so that the balls land in front of the players running behind them.
3. Players allow the balls to bounce only once before catching them.
4. Players continue jogging and the process continues each time you call out, "Now!"

Tips and Variations

- Double Jog Toss: Played the same as Jog Toss except that when a ball is tossed, the player two people behind the thrower is the one to catch the ball. Players will need to move quickly and exercise caution as they dodge the balls thrown by the players immediately in front of them.
- No-Bounce Jog Toss: Played the same as Jog Toss except that players must catch the ball in the air without letting it bounce. Be sure to use smaller balls for this version.
- For safety reasons remind players to keep their eyes on the balls they are catching so they do not get hit by a ball and possibly get injured. Fun chaos results.

Roll the Rails

Objective

To get the stability ball around the circle as many times as possible in one minute without the ball being "derailed"

Equipment

One stability ball per group

Number of Players

At least 10 players per group

Setup

- Players sit in a circle with each player alternating so that one player is pointing his feet into the circle and the next player is pointing her feet out of the circle. As players face each other, there should be enough room for the ball to roll over their legs without becoming stuck going against their bodies.
- Position a stability ball on the legs of two of the players.

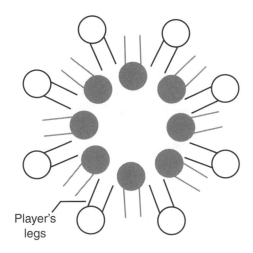

Player's
legs

Instructions

1. On your signal to begin, the players begin to move the ball around the circle of legs (or rails) using their hands.

2. Have the groups count each time they are successful at moving the ball around the circle.

3. If the ball goes outside the circle (or is "derailed"), one of the players retrieves the ball, and the group begins counting successive circles again from zero.

4. At the end of the time limit (one or two minutes), have the groups announce the highest number of successive circles they made.

Tips and Variations

Groups will learn that they will experience greater success with a steady, controlled pace than with an out-of-control, fast pace.

Pass the Egg

Objective

To move the stability ball around the circle as many times as possible in one minute

Equipment

One stability ball per group

Number of Players

Groups of at least four players

Setup

- With their knees up and feet flat on the floor, players lie in a circle and reach their hands over their heads to touch the toes of the players behind them.
- Give one player a stability ball.

Instructions

1. On your signal to begin, players move the ball around the circle by sitting up and passing it into the hands of the players in front of them.

2. Have the groups count each time they are successful at moving the ball around the circle.

3. If the ball falls off the hands, one of the players retrieves the ball, and the group begins counting successive circles again from zero.

4. At the end of one minute, have the groups announce the highest number of successive circles they made.

Tips and Variations

- This game gives students a fun and excellent way of doing sit-ups.

- Reverse Pass the Egg: Played the same as Pass the Egg except that the ball goes in the opposite direction. A player begins by sitting up and picking the ball off the hands of the player at his feet. That player lies back down, and the player behind him takes the ball off his hands.

- Turn Around and Switch Directions: Played the same as Pass the Egg except that after two full circles the players all turn to face the opposite direction and complete two more full circles before switching directions again. At the end of the time limit the groups announce the highest number of successive circles they made.

- Conveyor Belt: Played the same as Pass the Egg except that players lie in a straight line with the person at the front of the line holding the ball. Once a player passes the ball, he runs to the back of the line and waits for the next passing opportunity. Keep track of the time it takes groups to cross a room. (Do not play Conveyor Belt in a forward direction because the stability ball may bang someone's head against the ground if it is not caught.)

Eight-Beat Musical Routine

Objective

To develop an innovative dance routine using a stability ball

Equipment

- One stability ball per dancer
- CD (Choose music with a strong beat and clear eight count; marching tunes are great. For a kid-friendly CD with a good, strong beat, contact CIRA Ontario at www.ciraontario.com, and order their *Everybody Move* CD. Or call 905-575-2083.)
- CD player

Number of Players

Any number of players

Setup

Dancers are in a scattered position, each with a stability ball.

Instructions

1. Dancers listen to the music and develop an innovative routine for eight beats. All movements should coincide with the rhythm and beat of the music (players could skip a beat and go slower or go double-time).
2. Once dancers have perfected their routines, have them pair up and teach each other their routines so they can combine them for 16 beats of music. They should repeat their dances for every new 16 beats of music.
3. Once pairs of dancers have perfected their routines, have them join another dancing pair and teach each other their routines. They should repeat their dances for every new 32 beats of music for an entire song.
4. If you have time, have half the dancing groups watch the other half do their dances and then switch roles.

Tips and Variations

- Dance moves can involve regular exercises (push-ups or sit-ups with a stability ball), dance moves (grapevine or V steps while holding or bouncing the ball), sport moves (a shot in basketball or bowling or bouncing the ball around the body), or regular daily events (a morning stretch to the sky with hands up and holding the ball overhead or sitting on a bus seat [the ball] and bouncing up and down). Encourage the dancers to be creative with movements they are familiar with.

• Musical Groups: In groups of four, each dancer with a ball, dancers develop movements with the ball for 32 beats of music. The group then repeats these movements for 32 beats for the rest of the song. Dance moves can be as simple as bouncing the ball with one or two hands, or can involve more complex actions such as bounce passing the ball to a neighbor on the left or passing the ball across a circle.

Watermelon Toss

Objective

To get the stability ball around the circle as many times as possible in one minute without the ball landing on the ground

Equipment

One stability ball per group

Number of Players

Groups of at least four players

Setup

- Players stand in a circle, facing the middle, at least one pace apart. The farther apart players stand from each other, the more difficult the game is.
- Give one player a stability ball.

Instructions

1. On your signal to begin, the first player tosses the ball to the player next to her.
2. Have the groups count each time they are successful at moving the ball around the circle.
3. If the ball falls on the ground, one of the players retrieves the ball, and the group begins counting successive circles again from zero.
4. At the end of the time limit (one or two minutes), have the groups announce the highest number of successive circles they made.

Tips and Variations

- Double Watermelon Toss: Played the same as Watermelon Toss except that groups use two stability balls.
- Increase the distance players stand apart (possibly add one bounce to each pass).
- Use a BOSU Ballast Ball to make catching more challenging.

Feet Pass

Objective

To use the feet to pass the stability ball around the circle as many times as possible in a set amount of time without the ball touching the ground

Equipment

One stability ball per group

Number of Players

Groups of four to six players

Setup

- Players sit in a circle, facing the middle, about one pace apart (you may have them begin closer together at first).
- Give one player a stability ball.

Instructions

1. On your signal to begin, the first player lifts the ball between her legs and passes it to the next player's legs.
2. Have the groups count each time they are successful at moving the ball around the circle.
3. If the ball touches the ground, the group begins counting successive circles again from zero.
4. At the end of the time limit (one or two minutes), have the groups announce the highest number of successive circles they made.

Tips and Variations

Two-Ball Feet Pass: Played the same as Feet Pass except that groups pass two balls around their circles at the same time.

Circular Moving Sidewalk

Objective

To get the stability ball around the circle as many times as possible in one minute without the ball falling off the sidewalk

Equipment

One stability ball per group

Number of Players

At least 10 players per group

Setup

- Players lie in a circle in alternating directions (i.e., every other player lies with her feet inside the circle and the others lie with their feet outside the circle).
- Players put their hands up.
- Position a stability ball on the hands of two of the players.

Instructions

1. On your signal to begin, the players begin to move the ball around the circle of hands.
2. Have the groups count each time they are successful at moving the ball around the circle.
3. If the ball falls off the hands, one of the players retrieves the ball, and the group begins counting successive circles again from zero.
4. At the end of the time limit (one or two minutes), have the groups announce the highest number of successive circles they made.

Tips and Variations

- Straight Moving Sidewalk: Played the same as Circular Moving Sidewalk except that players lie in a straight line rather than in a circle and move to the end of the line once they have passed the ball. Players measure how far the line can move without losing the ball.
- Groups will learn that they will experience greater success with a steady, controlled pace than with an out-of-control, fast pace.

Gutter Ball

Objective

To roll a stability ball between players the most successive times in a set amount of time

Equipment

One stability ball per group

Number of Players

Groups of 12 to 30 players

Setup

- Players in each group stand in a double circle facing each other, with twice as many players on the outside circle (facing in) as on the inside circle.
- Give one player the ball at an assigned start spot.

Instructions

1. On your signal to begin, the players pass the ball between the circles.
2. Have the groups count each successive time the ball goes past the start spot in a certain amount of time (one minute should be more than adequate).

Tips and Variations

Players will find it advantageous to stand close together.

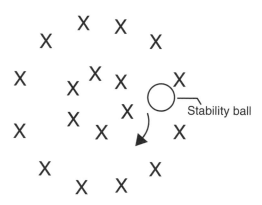

Stability ball

7

Team Games

Good old-fashioned team games are great for helping young people be active and have fun. The team games in this chapter have some significant twists to ensure that *everyone* stays active and finds the activity enjoyable. Games include Cat and Mouse, in which teams try to catch one stability ball with another, and Not in My House, in which balls are constantly coming into players' homes as they are just as actively throwing them out.

Balls Away

Objective

To move the stability ball past the opponent's scoring line by throwing tennis balls at it

Equipment

- One stability ball per 10 to 15 players
- 50 tennis balls per 10 to 15 players
- Tape for scoring lines, unless suitable lines are already on the floor

Number of Players

Ten to 15 players per stability ball

Setup

- Place the ball in the middle of the playing area.
- Tape parallel scoring lines approximately three to five paces from either side of the ball.
- Place parallel restraining lines approximately two to three paces beyond the scoring lines.
- Divide the players into two teams and have each team go behind its restraining line.
- Give each team 25 tennis balls.

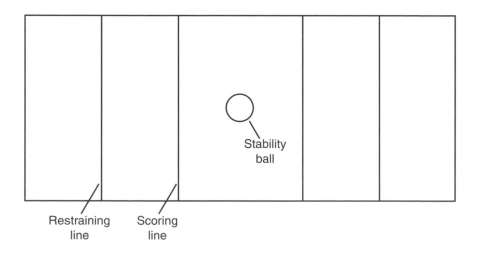

Restraining line   Scoring line   Stability ball

Instructions

1. On your signal to begin, players begin throwing tennis balls at the stability ball in an effort to get the ball to move past their opponents' scoring lines.
2. Players may retrieve tennis balls in front of the restraining line, but can only throw at the stability ball from behind the restraining line.
3. Players may not block the opposing team from hitting the ball, nor may they contact the stability ball in front of the restraining line.
4. A point is scored when the stability ball rolls past a scoring line. At that point, return the ball to the center and instruct players to resume play. At the end of a specified time, the team with the most points wins.

Tips and Variations

- If you have a large group, use extra stability balls and tennis balls.
- Place a BOSU Ballast Ball in the middle and, instead of using tennis balls, use other stability balls to move it from the center.
- If using all stability balls, designate one or two players from each team to retrieve the balls from the middle area.

Cat and Mouse

Objective

For the cat ball to catch the mouse ball

Equipment

Two stability balls of different colors

Number of Players

At least two teams of at least eight players (having more players per team is preferable)

Setup

- Separate players into two teams, and have each player select a partner on her team.
- Players stand in a double circle facing their partners, alternating pairs from the two teams (i.e., a mouse team pair stands beside a cat team pair).
- Assign the cat ball to one team and the mouse ball to the other.

Instructions

1. The cat team can only touch the cat ball, and the mouse team can only touch the mouse ball. Either ball can contact players from either team accidentally, but players may not purposely slow down or speed up the ball of the other team.
2. On your signal to begin, the cat team tries to propel its ball around the circle so that it catches up with the mouse ball.

Key:
X = Team A
O = Team B
Ⓒ = Cat ball
Ⓜ = Mouse ball

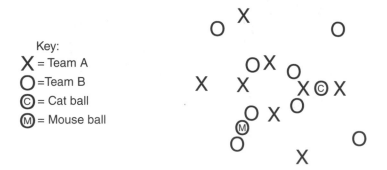

3. The mouse team tries to keep its ball away from the cat ball.

4. The leader times how long it takes for the cat to catch the mouse.

5. Switch roles (the cat team becomes the mouse team and vice versa).

Tips and Variations

- Figure-Eight Cat and Mouse: Played the same as Cat and Mouse except that instead of having one circle, have two circles with an opening at one side that joins the two circles.
- Two-Mice Figure-Eight Cat and Mouse: Played the same as Figure-Eight Cat and Mouse except that there are two mice.
- Cloverleaf Cat and Mouse: Played the same as Cat and Mouse except that instead of having one circle, have three circles with an opening at the side that joins the three circles.
- Two- (or Three-) Mice Cloverleaf Cat and Mouse: Played the same as Cloverleaf Cat and Mouse except that there are two or three mice.

Lapping the Ball

Objective

To run more laps than the other team

Equipment

One stability ball

Number of Players

Two teams of 5 to 30 players

Setup

- One team lines up with players facing the backs of their teammates. The player at the front of this line holds a stability ball. This group is the throwing team.
- The other team is in a scattered position in the playing area. This group is the retrieving team.

Instructions

1. The player with the ball tosses it to a place where there are few retrieving players.
2. The entire throwing team does jumping jacks while the player at the end of the line runs around the entire team. When the running player returns to her starting spot, she tags the second player on the back. The second player then runs around the entire team, and when she returns to her spot, she tags the third player on the back. The throwing team tries to get as many people as possible to run a lap before the retrieving team completes its task.
3. The retrieving team gets the stability ball as quickly as possible and forms a line with the player who retrieved the ball at the front with the ball. The retrieving player passes the ball over her head to the player behind. That player pushes it under her legs to the next player, who passes it over her head to the next player, who pushes it under her legs, and so on. Players alternate passing over and under until the last player in line holds the ball. When the last player in line gets the ball, she shouts, "Stop!"
4. On the shout of stop, the throwing team calls out how many players completed a lap.
5. The two teams switch roles.
6. Have the players continue the game until each team has retrieved the ball three to five times.

Tips and Variations

Specify various exercises for the throwing team, such as marching or hopping around the group, or counting the number of can-can kicks or sit-ups the entire group can do. Specify various challenges for the retrieving team, such as passing the ball down the left side of the line and returning on the right, or over and under to the back of the group and back to the front again, or rolling the ball between the whole team's legs and returning the ball to the front overhead.

Crab Soccer

Objective

To score more goals than the opponents

Equipment

- One stability ball per game
- Four cones to identify two goals

Number of Players

Two teams of 5 to 10 players

Setup

- Set up a playing area with goals five paces wide at either end.
- Each team is in a scattered position in its half of the playing area. Each team has one goalie in the goal area. All players are in a crab position on the floor (backs toward the floor and walking on hands and feet).

Instructions

1. Throw the ball down the middle of the playing area to begin play.
2. Players may kick the ball, but may not advance the ball with their hands. If a player advances the ball with his hands, the other team gets the ball at that location and has a free kick—which means the kicker can kick the ball uncontested. Once the ball is kicked, play resumes as normal.
3. A goal is scored when the ball goes between the two cones and the bottom of the ball is no higher than the height of the ball above the floor.
4. When a team scores, have the teams return to their respective halves and throw the ball down the middle again.

Tips and Variations

- Two-Ball Crab Soccer: Played the same as Crab Soccer except that the teams use two balls (this is a good alternative if you have many players).
- Regular Indoor Soccer: Played the same as regular indoor soccer but uses a stability ball instead of a soccer ball.
- Snow Soccer: If you have a soccer field nearby and lots of snow, have players dress for the outdoors and play a regular game of soccer using one or more stability balls instead of a soccer ball.

Hoops

Objective

To score more hoops than the opponents

Equipment

- One hula hoop per team
- One stability ball
- Tape to mark two circles

Number of Players

Two teams of three to six players

Setup

- At either end of the floor, mark out a circle or square approximately four to five paces in diameter (a basketball circle or key will work).
- One player from each team goes into this circle or square and holds a hula hoop.
- The other players are in a scattered position around the playing area.

Instructions

This game is played like basketball with the following exceptions:
- Players score points by throwing the ball through a hoop held by one of his or her team's players.
- Players can dribble the ball with both hands.
- If a defensive player is fouled, the defensive team gets the ball. If an offensive player is fouled, the offensive team gets an automatic hoop, and the defensive team gets the ball.

Tips and Variations

None

Not in My House

Objective

To have the fewest balls in one's "house" at the end of the game

Equipment

Approximately one stability ball per player

Number of Players

Any number of players

Setup

- Divide a playing area into two courts (or "houses").
- Divide the players into two teams, and direct players to scatter themselves throughout their houses.
- Divide the balls equally between the two teams.

Instructions

1. On your signal to start, players begin to throw, kick, roll, or use any other means of propelling the stability balls out of their house and into the other team's house. However, all balls must hit the ground once in the team's house before going into the opponent's house. (This is done for safety considerations.)
2. Players cannot leave their house.
3. At a time you have determined, call, "Stop." Have each team count the number of balls in its house.
4. Congratulate the winners and quickly start a new game, but vary the stop times (one game might be 20 seconds long, another might be 10 seconds long, another might be 60 seconds long). Many games and quick starts ensure that players will focus more on the activity than on the score.

Tips and Variations

*   Tactically (and for safety reasons), it is advantageous for players to throw the balls where opposing players are not—the balls will roll farther into the opponent's house.
*   Four-Team Not in My House: Played the same as Not in My House except that there are four teams and the room is divided into quadrants.

Keep Away in My House

Objective

To make as many consecutive passes as possible without having the ball stolen

Equipment

One stability ball per game

Number of Players

Two teams of four to six players

Setup

- Divide a playing area into two courts (or "houses").
- Each team goes into its house.
- Give one team a stability ball.
- The team that does not have the stability ball sends two thieves into the other team's house to try to steal the ball.

Instructions

1. The team that has the ball passes it around and tries to complete as many consecutive passes as possible.
2. The two thieves from the opposing team try to steal the ball and pass it to their teammates waiting in their house.
3. If the ball is stolen, the thieves return to their house and that team tries to get as many consecutive passes as possible, while the team that has just been stolen from sends two thieves over and tries to steal the ball back.
4. Thieves may not take the ball from someone who is holding the ball; they can steal the ball only once it has been thrown.
5. Players holding the ball have five seconds to pass it—otherwise, the ball is given to the other team.
6. Players holding the ball may pivot on one foot only and may not otherwise walk or run while in possession of the ball.

Tips and Variations

Regular Keep Away With Four Players: One player is It, and the other three players try to pass the ball to each other without the It intercepting the ball. The player holding the ball cannot walk or run with the ball. If the It intercepts the ball, the last person to throw the ball becomes the new It.

Bouncing Body Ball

Adapted, by permission, from GT Educational Inc. Available: www.bodyballgame.com

Objective

To score points by throwing a Body Ball onto the special vest of the team's catcher

Equipment

- One stability ball per player
- One Body Ball per game
- Two Body Ball vests per game

Number of Players

Two teams of five to nine players each

Setup

- Define a court (a volleyball court works well). The ends of the court are the end lines.
- Divide players into two teams of five to nine players.
- Have each team select one player to be its catcher. Give the catcher a vest and position her behind her team's end line.
- Each team starts at the other team's end line.
- Give a Body Ball to a player on one of the teams.
- Each player sits on a stability ball.

Instructions

1. On your signal to begin, the offensive players attempt to pass the Body Ball to teammates, with the goal of tossing the Body Ball so that it sticks to the vest of the team's catcher. The defensive team tries to intercept or knock down the pass from the offensive team. When that happens, the defensive team gets the ball.
2. Players move about the court by bouncing on their stability balls.
3. When a team scores a point, the catcher gives the ball to a member of the other team, and play resumes.
4. If a pass goes incomplete (or is knocked down or intercepted by the other team), the other team gets the ball where its player picks it up. The team that lost the ball cannot touch the ball until it is passed by the player who picks the ball up.

Tips and Variations

- Key Bouncing Body Ball: Played the same as Bouncing Body Ball except that teams use a court that resembles a basketball court. The catchers are positioned in the basketball key. No one else may enter the basketball key.

- To order Body Balls and Body Ball vests, and for additional information, go to www.bodyballgame.com.

Ultimate Stability Ball

Objective
To touch a stability ball against the opponent's wall

Equipment
One small stability ball per game

Number of Players
Two teams of three to five players

Setup

- Two teams stand within 1 yard or meter of their walls.
- A player on one of the teams holds the ball.

Instructions

1. When the two teams are ready, the player with the ball begins play by throwing it to the other team.
2. The other team runs forward to get the ball.
3. When a player has the ball, he may pivot on one foot but may not walk or run with the ball.
4. The team with the ball attempts to pass the ball to a player who can touch it against the wall to score a point. The ball has to travel at least 2 yards or meters with each pass. Once a team has scored a point, the game begins anew with the scoring team throwing the ball to the opposing team in the same way the game was begun.
5. Players on the defensive team cannot get closer than 2 yards or meters to a player holding the ball; from that distance they must try to intercept the passed ball.
6. If a ball is dropped or an incomplete pass is made, the other team takes possession of the ball from the place where they retrieve it.

Tips and Variations

Add another stability ball when more players participate. When a point is scored, both teams line up as they did at the beginning of the game, and each team throws a ball to the other team.

Fit Circle

Objective

To be the first team to pass the ball from the first player to the last player and then back to the first player

Equipment

One stability ball per team

Number of Players

Teams of 5, 7, 9, 11, or 15 players

Setup

- Each team stands in a circle with players at least two paces apart.
- Give one player in each team a stability ball.

Instructions

1. On your signal to begin, the players with the balls bounce pass them to the players two players to the right.
2. Teams continue passing the balls two players to the right until the first player gets the ball back. When the first player gets the ball, the team jumps up and down and calls out, "We did it! We did it!"
3. The first team to complete the task is the winner.

Tips and Variations

- Two-Ball Fit Circle: Played the same as Fit Circle except that the first player passes one ball, then grabs a second ball (and a third, if desired) and passes that. When the first player gets the last ball, the team jumps up and down and calls out, "We did it! We did it!"
- Everyone-With-a-Ball Fit Circle: Played the same as Fit Circle except that everyone begins with a ball. One player has a different sized or colored ball so the group knows when all players have their balls back.

About the Author

John Byl, PhD, is a professor of education at Redeemer University College in Ancaster, Ontario, Canada, where he teaches the Teaching of Elementary School Health and Physical Education course. The author or coauthor of 10 books on health and games for children, Dr. Byl has been a high school teacher or university professor since 1977 and has recently coauthored a book titled *Christian Paths to Health and Wellness.* He has led numerous workshops on games and fitness for children at fitness conferences and in educational settings.

Dr. Byl is the president of CIRA (Canadian Intramural Recreation Association) Ontario, an organization that promotes fun, active participation for all. He has received numerous awards, including a Literary Award from the Christian Society for Kinesiology and Leisure Studies (CSKLS) and a Presidential Award, which recognizes those who have displayed actions compatible with the mission of the CSKLS.

When he's not busy teaching or writing, he loves playing active games with his grandchildren and keeping active himself by cycling, jogging, and golfing.